THE ART OF COMING UNDONE

THE ART OF COMING UNDONE

CHRISTIE COLLINS

ARTWORK BY ERNA KUIK

THE **BLACK SPRING**
PRESS GROUP

First published in 2023
by The Black Spring Press Group
Maida Vale Publishing imprint
Maida Vale, London W9,
United Kingdom

Typeset with graphic design by Edwin Smet

ISBN 9781915406200

*The editor has generally followed American spelling and punctuation
at the author's request.*

BLACKSPRINGPRESSGROUP.COM

For my mother, Kathy Collins.
&
For my dear friend, Lauren Dodd.

NOTE TO THE READER

This collection includes an ekphrastic collaboration between American poet Christie Collins and Dutch artist Erna Kuik. The collaboration comprises 11 poem/image pairings. When reading this book, the images correspond to the poems that directly follow them. Half of the images by Erna were created based on Christie's poems; the other half of the images were used by Christie as inspiration for the poems.

TABLE OF CONTENTS

I want to insist that female pain is still news. It's always news.
We've never already heard it… The wounded woman gets called
a stereotype, and sometimes she is. But sometimes she's just true.
— Leslie Jamison, *Grand Unified Theory of Female Pain*

I believed in him, he believed in me, then we
grew, and grew, I grieved him, he grieved me…
I did not leave him, he did not leave me,
I freed him, he freed me.
— Sharon Olds, from *Stag's Leap*

Love is first an element,
an atmosphere, a milky cloud.

Out of the cloud a face appears,
and then a word.
— Jeremy Hooker, from *Ancestral Lines*

LAW OF LOSING

What happens to the fusion
      of a love that's been lost,
knowing that *energy cannot*
      be created or destroyed?

Where does love reemerge – after?
      At the end-of-love museum?
I have so many exhibits there.

SUMMER BLUES

All summer long, I filled bowl after bowl with blueberries,
dreamed of running off through tall fields of sugar cane.
My body bloomed once that year, a bright pink azalea born
of the spring, singed by the Louisiana summer that welts
even the softest kiss, sweats out desire like flood water.
I laid back on the hot earth, a bed of flowers under my figure
or was it the dog's red blanket fresh from the dryer?
I burned in the backyard and at the public pool, the lenses
on my sunglasses as dark as Medea's heart, if she had one.
Dark and round so no one could see in, see me, but
still I squinted my eyes to the sun, tight as raisins.
That summer, I ate blueberries in bulk, buoyed
each bowlful on my ceramic chest, which floated
boat-to-ocean on the tide of my breath, a water-logged
copy of *Play It As It Lays* by my side. I considered each berry,
pressed each to my lips, rolled each like a lonely planet
between my fingers. I longed to feel my breasts, my back
in a bath of berries, to drown, to rot in sweetness.
I dreamed of buying a bushel of my own. That summer
I didn't know Wednesday from the weekend,
each day a different shade of the same strange color.
I prayed to God, thankful for abundance. I prayed to God
that he would take it all away. I decided that such prayers
were decadent, wicked, so I prayed again for forgiveness.
That Joan Didion summer asked me to pit myself
in exchange for passion, and I did so willingly, willingly.
I traced the route to Albuquerque in coral lipstick, which
on the map looked like the curve of an unsure smile.
I cried when I didn't leave, threw each Kleenex,
each origami wad of despair to the blue paper sky.
I kept my sunglasses tight on the bridge of my nose
as my mother taught me to hide the tears, the circles.

I burned, palms to the sun. I ate on, prayed on.
I ate the thick, sweet berries and said *ready.*
I ate the small, bitter berries and said *not right.*
When my hand reached for more and came back full,
my mouth could only mutter: *empty, empty, empty.*

HONEYBEES

How could I not have grieved?

When their bodies poisoned into a deep
and enduring sleep, drifted like
dusty snowflakes from the attic above.
Down, down to rest on the linoleum
floor in my therapist's bathroom.

When it took the maintenance crew
hours to undo their nests,
the impressive sheets of comb
that had been so carefully
constructed of homespun wax, saliva.

When the wealth of their honey –
that golden sea, their life's work –
was carelessly drained from the combs
into several black waste bags.

When I witnessed their wings,
the capsules of their precious bodies –
head, thorax, abdomen – stepped on,
crunched, swept up, disposed of.

When such a bustling city as it must
have been fell & fell silent.

As the afternoon backbends into night,
I fashion the memory of their wings
into words, arrange them into the slow
language of loss I'm learning to speak.
I write *HOW TO SURVIVE?*
in my wellness journal, stare out
of the open window, listening for answers.

FIRST LOVE

Poem-of-mine,
here we are parked

at Make-Out Point.
In the front seats

of my daddy's
red hot Firebird,

the summer burns
on your breath

& because I feel
luck or lust,

I peel the cotton
straps of your tank

top from your
shoulders & kiss

the soft sounds
of your long lines.

I want to scan
my tongue over

the curves of your
form. I feel frisky,

so I go to cop a feel
of your images, but

you turn me down,
taking my hand away

from the very cusp
of short-lived splendor.

I'm moving too fast
you say & clumsily,

grabbing at anything.
Forcing it, you say.

The night has turned,
my thinking revised.

The moonlight glares,
illuminating the refrain

between us. Your face
a soft lyric, an elegy.

Other couples peel
out, late for curfew.

What truth to take
from this blunder?

That this was just
a messy fling, a mistake,

soon to be buried
in attic notebooks?

At your doorstep, you
reach for my hands,

kiss my forehead,
and assure me this

is only the beginning –
that you will unfold

when you are ready,
when I am ready,

when the conceit
is finally well-crafted.

My heartbeat slows.
I nod, peck your cheek,

begin the lifelong drive
towards getting it right.

GIRL TALK

My ragdoll decides my fate:
  she says my love for him is soft
    like a wet noodle handshake.

If I were you, she tells me,
  I'd man up.
  I'd stop pussy-footin'.
  I'd seal the deal.

She lights a Winston Red
  & pours Glen Elgin single malt
    into a doll-sized tumbler.

It's a typical Tuesday night:
  the hours pass vacant, cautious, dignified.
    What I've left unspoken forms
    deep rivers in my waking,
    deep rivers sing my dreams to sleep.

My ragdoll positions an Elvis Costello record on the
turntable
  as she clips her difficult toenails.
    From her perch on the bookshelf,
    she grins at the polite distance that's kept,
    she grins at the words I'll never say aloud.

Where do your thoughts come from? I ask.
  How can you see the world clearly
    with your crooked button eyes?

She leans forward, tossing a nail clipping
        toward my face. It lands on my lip.
                I'd grow a pair, she continues.
                I'd hit it & quit it.

Some plight between pride & passion
        compels me to climb onto the bookshelf
                & reach for her arm:

With that touch, my head goes limp,
        my hands turn to cloth & it's she
                who jumps down, steps into my jeans,
                & grabs my keys on her way out the door.

        She says she's going to find him
                & kiss him till it hurts.

ANOTHER NIGHT ON BOURBON STREET

On Bourbon Street, we fall into Tropical Isle,
where we order Hand Grenades, sip the electric
mix of iced green syrup and booze into our
already unsteady bodies. They detonate midway
down, blasting the afternoon into fire, jazz,
gaslight, yet another untold story of desire.
I arm-wrestle the bartender. He lets me win
even though I said not to. My prize: a tiny
plastic alligator he places on my palm, right
on the crossroads of my life line, my love line.
Enter: a hooded figure with long, sharp fingernails.
Exit: Mindy's bright pink bachelorette party.
Enter: a winged cockroach who will never fly.
Exit: the five of us back onto the tightrope streets.
Where Iberville crosses Bourbon, a mule turns
my way, turns his whole frame to face me.
I half expect him to bow. I half expect him
to offer me a ride away from all that binds us.
But he is harnessed to a carriage. His master
gives me a carrot. I feed him. I stare into his eye,
bronze and aflame with all the words, the choices
I most fear. When the evening buzzes in
on the mosquito's wings, blood dripping
from its proboscis, my head is all third eyeball.
I am pared down to my most basic: thorax, thirst.
We're all villain and victim here.

WHOLE NINE YARDS

Local police called when a woman, 52, was seen tending to her garden
topless, wearing only a bright yellow thong and pink gloves,
reports the Arizona Daily Star.

No one mentions the yard unless the weather
is mild & warm. Yard leaps from word
to memory, dead like clay, until dug up again.

I say the world does not die.
I say it takes a woman to build a world.

What girl didn't dream of a secret garden:
a green moor, an English mansion,
stone walls & eyes that peek.

What woman would deny the wind
on her bare form?

This is intimacy:
saying yes to mean yes.

I've been the seed & the shovel.
I've been sized & shipped.

I've been green like turnip,
white as the skin on the onion.

I've been all colors, lover,
& the best one is free.

DEAR DEPRESSION

you hang threadbare
        like another woman's
death, the single apartment,
        the passing days,
the altar, empty at noon,
        you cruel rusted
hooks, opulent thorns,
& *what have you done all day?*

you cotton mouth,
        you burned-up
memory, tragedy of
        radiance, you dark
circles, tired shoulders,
& *could this just be low vitamin D?*

you torn palaces,
        you single hairpin
in tangled coils,
        you mouth of static,
you lackluster, lacking,
        you cold flame,
& *shouldn't you go outside?*
You'd feel better if you went outside.

THE RUMBLE

I once drove from Missouri to Alabama –
spring-boarded through four states –
with a bullet between my teeth.
I was a rocket, a weapon on the move.

Spring-boarded through four states,
I found two four-leaf clovers by my car.
I was a rocket, a weapon on the move.
My thoughts ballooned with uncertainty.

I picked the two four-leaf clovers, wore
them as eyes. All I saw was luck.
My dreams deflated with indecision
at the intersection of desire and duty.

All I saw was luck gone bad, gone wrong.
But, when I could've driven anywhere then
from the intersection of desire and duty,
      I drove to you, duty dear.

OVARIAN TERATOMA

A tumor capable of growing hair, teeth, and other body parts.

Teratoma didn't receive invite to your tea party.
Teratoma don't like tea cakes.
Teratoma has three teeth, a patch of slimy hair,
          and a baby foot growing off to one side.
Teratoma thinks he looks fat in jeans.
Teratoma hungry for cardboard.
Teratoma has no eye but if he had eye
          he'd blink twice for yes.
Teratoma eat his twin.
Teratoma don't like mirrors.
Teratoma come from body but has no
          mother to speak of.
Teratoma see the world in white.
Teratoma likes to spin.
Teratoma want to wear icicles as earrings,
          but in the body, icicles melt.
Teratoma has an itch on his noggin.
Teratoma want to feel the sunlight.
Teratoma another wonder of the body,
          but he knows you look away.

DEAR BLUE PILL

Can I call you *Bill?*
Seems easier, more casual.

Did you like what I did there, Bill —
using two of your descriptors to create

a neologism, a portmanteau?
By calling you Bill, I mean

to poke fun at your unwelcomed
presence. No, Bill, that's a lie.

I mean to keep you up at night,
writhing, waiting for me to find you

as an equal in a dimly lit alley.
But you are not a Bill, a *you.*

You are a reaping, a lasso
wound into incandescence,

a small bandage stretched tight
over a harvest of tissue,

neurons. Bill, if I can call you
Bill, you are sent to make

nice, to untwine, to wrangle
a wild, sad mind, and so

I'm warning you, Bill.
I'm keeping my distance

as I take you into my body,
as you move unwanted

about my bloodstream.
Don't get too comfortable,

Bill, because when you least
expect a storm, I will be

the thunder whipping
outside your locked door,

the branches breaking apart,
the clothesline snapped in two.

ME TOO

At thirty I scream
      ME TOO because at twenty
            they said to whisper.

HOW TO LEAVE YOUR HUSBAND

The only way to leave your husband is to know
without a doubt that you can't not leave.

Turn unfeeling, at first. Otherwise, you won't be able
to go through with it: the near-impossible work of parting.
Turn into a whirlwind who simply completes tasks.
Turn dead-brained, unforgivably efficient.

Move into your friend's vacant studio apartment
where the only single bed is inside the closet.
This will be your summer home, tiny but filled
with art and color. Tiny but yours alone
to breathe. To catch up with yourself.

Teach the craft of poetry to a sect of retired nuns.
Allow them to teach you about perennial flowers,
about harnessing faith in one's convictions.

Dance in the living room, drink red wine, eat cheap
take-out from La Salvadoreña across the street.
Enjoy your last summer in Louisiana, the mossy
live oaks, the carnival sun, the long-necked egrets.

When it comes time to move abroad, buy the boxes,
the tape, the bubble wrap. Rent the storage unit.

Pack up the rest of your old house. Sign your name
on the wall of what used to be your closet. Thank
the house for being the first dwelling in your life
to feel like home. Know that places stay with you.

Do not allow yourself to think of your husband alone
in that house at night, your seat on the couch empty.
Or your dog watching the door, his ears perking up
at each car that passes. These thoughts will break you.

Do not allow yourself to take the blame for what
it took two people to break. Do not stay broken
for the benefit of someone else. What you don't know

at this moment is that he will move on soon.
Sooner than you ever thought possible.
You will be forced to learn that the person who leaves
can also be the last to let go. The one who grieves the most.

So, get on the plane. Cross an ocean. Trust yourself.
Trust your hunger. Trust that life isn't supposed to hurt.

NESTING

At first,
you loved the open cage of me,
the lightning embrace of me.

You loved the skin-soft curves,
the creases of me. The flighty
free will of me. The home
in my own skin of me.

Home. You wanted to home
with me, in my skin with me,
in a nest of twigs & pine with me.
To winter & spring with me.

But, from our nest, you didn't
like the wildness of me,
the changing plumes of me,
the strong-scared songs of me.

What's left of you, your love
of me – a crown of nettles,
which settles in my hair.
The birds – they poke, they prod
at me, singing the loneliest song –
of me, of me, of me.

KINTSUGI

Now that we are over,
over and placed aside
like a pressed flower in a bible,
I'm tempted to ask *am I better?*
But, just as I think the question,
another seismic shift cracks my skin.
A part of me breaks off onto the floor.
Like a split fruit, I will never be
whole again. *An object in motion tends
to stay in motion.* The science of my
body actuates the laws of physics.
I stay in motion: breaking, willing
the parts back together, carrying
myself in my own arms as one
carries firewood to a furnace.
I carry myself from one fear
or folly to the next. One mantra
to the next. Still, I shouldn't
think to ask myself *am I better?*
That's the answer you would
demand, even now.

WALKING SPANISH

How fast your body follows mine – this much I know.
The pair of us hopping into a taxi after a hot rain,
the evening sun slipping through the eye of Cerro de la Silla.
We became friends that night, do you remember?
My wet fingers thumbing through a tiny red dictionary,
looking for the Spanish word for *beer*. Our faces damp with rain.

I know too the way you take pictures from the back of a moving van
of the desert hills, a blooming cactus, an abandoned
shanty house, two turtles in combat. The pictures you took of me,
one with our faces so close I pursed my lips from nerves.

The way you sang along with our summer students
from the back of the school bus,
your lips mouthing *Una Salinas, Dos Salinas…*
The thrill of going in your direction.

I know the formality of your figure on a plane.
How you inspect the wings. How you love the rushing speed.
How easy it's always been between us
as long as I didn't say it, didn't ask if we were *more*.

Then, when it all changed years later
and we were ill-timed lovers, I came to know
the swift, tight angles your arm and foot
make in tandem as you shift the gears,
a gesture wholly your own, as you sailed
us down from the mountains,
sand still on our toes, the lake lingering in our ears,
the convection of the air through the window
cooling a heat that left us both scared and smiling.

I've known torque firsthand, have measured my body's
reaction to the force of you. You were the axis, the pivot point.
I was the object, the girl turning, turning with desire.

I've known the way you feel in my arms
outside the airport when you must go. I must stay.
The same feeling you always stir when you
are in the air above me, leaving contrails in your wake.
Your memory a flash of heat transfer
always just overhead, always a trace of you in my skies.

I have known the combustion of a long goodbye,
the way it burns over and over.

HOW TO BUILD A DOCK

Block out three summers,
buy a forest of Western Red Cedar.

Prepare for failure, the kind you must
dive under water to amend.

Use string to measure the distance between
posts or the distance from start to finish.

Be the lover whose song cannot be cured.
Be the girl whose father wouldn't approve.

Only when you finish will you know
the depth of your futile desires:

here, at the edge of the dock,
you are surrounded by saltwater, but you
are no closer to knowing the sea.

GLORY

While waiting in line to pay for gas in an overstocked service
station, who has not been tempted to purchase one

of those one-dollar grab bags bundled in brown paper
and bottom heavy like a packed lunch? You don't need

another oversized *I Love Florida* tee shirt or a sand-filled
keychain, but the suspense is surprisingly unwholesome.

Something like the lure of online dating. You said you wouldn't,
but you've thought about those deep levels of compatibility

advertised on late night infomercials. You know about
being dimensional. You've kissed with your eyes open.

You want what you want. Or you want to know what you want.
It's the experience that counts, which is why, when you go pee

in the truckstop bathroom next door, you stop and study
the round hole in the wall that's just even with your waist.

You want to be someone else or the someone you really are,
so you place your open mouth to the wall and close your eyes.

SINGING RAIN

Our bodies formed into a séance circle
in Pirate Alley, the tour guide weaves the tale
of Dagobert and legend of the Singing Rain.
A light shower starts to fall onto the dark streets
lit by the pearlescent moon. A lone street violinist
plucks his strings in the wet evening air, composing
a melody of quarter notes and quandaries.

The last time we were in New Orleans together,
I picked an azalea in City Park, wore its pink bloom
behind my ear. I was all emotion, a woman first wise
to fulfilled desire, to the long-awaited possibility of you.
We were younger than we thought at the time.
We wanted more. We took it. We didn't consider
that it takes more than *wanting*, no matter how much.

Tonight, we learn that Dagobert, a priest, retrieved
the bodies of dead rebels who'd been denied
a proper funeral and burial, led a procession
of their bodies to the graveyard, singing as he labored,
leaving traces of his song on the nighttime rainfall
here in this lonesome alley. With his voice came salvation.
With his voice came peace and new beginnings.

Tonight, this city welcomes us again, forgives
but refuses to forget. This city with its old folktales,
the gas lanterns, the heat, the horses and carriages,
the street weddings – it's the right place to admit love.
And the right place to bury love lost, here at sea level
or in a crowded cemetery where the sun turns skin to ash.

Tonight, the voice of Dagobert in the deluge, calling
home the otherwise damned. Tonight, rain-soaked,
haunted, and with nowhere at present to call home,
I'm finally ready to be angry and to be resolved.
I'm finally ready to number my sacrifices.
I'm finally ready to walk away, to shed the story of us.

DEAR READER, LOVE POET

I have a theory that no poem
sounds like a bad poem,

provided that the knowing poet
has taken time to practice reading

the verse aloud, visualizing the valleys
of syllables in each word, breathing

in just the right corners, following the line
breaks like a trail through the woods.

For all we know, a giraffe might stumble
into this poem. He might unfurl his long black

tongue against a toddler's rosy cheek, and if
you hear this image aloud, you can see the long,

spotted neck of the animal. It doesn't cross your
mind to judge if one can *get away with* writing

a poem about a giraffe. It's already been done
and here you are at the zoo participating

in the tenderness of this moment, this world,
this strange existence feeling smaller, kinder.

If the reader is prepared & passionate,
certainly any poem could be moving, which

is why I wish I could be there with you
now as you read this line to yourself.

I want to go back to the beginning & read
this poem to you because in hearing it,

I would give you a small piece of myself
which would break from my voice into flight.

As I read, you would hear undercurrents,
a brave passion. In all honesty, you might

hear me slip or stammer on a word because
that happens sometimes as do other truths

when I let go of this tight grip, when I let
the robe slip off my shoulders, when it's just me

and my voice in front of the stage lights,
the audience waiting.

OUT OF DATE

I must seem to you now
an itch for which
no ointment will soothe.

A hangnail your teeth
work – mouth to finger –
to excise, spit out.

A project, gone wrong,
babbling of its own failure.

I must seem to you now
a pothole every mile or so,
tearing into your tomorrow.

A bad oyster, out-of-date,
despite the earnest pearl.

THE KIND THING, THE DUTIFUL THING

Your emails now end *Thanks.* Full stop.
I've been relegated to a person no closer
to you than a client, an acquaintance. Your
messages have shortened, become less frequent.
I know soon they will stop coming altogether.
But, I won't forget the day we buried our beloved
calico, Lucy, between the 2nd and 3rd posts
in our backyard. For weeks, I'd been giving
her at-home hospice care: hand-feeding her, cleaning
her, moving her into the sunlight. Despite the odds,
she went on eating and purring, even when she could
no longer walk, when her once rotund body hollowed.
Dad said that's what love will do. He meant the healing
powers of connection prolonging the inevitable.
We agonized over what love meant in this moment.
When it came time for that long ride to the vet
it was Dad again who told us this choice, this act
was the kind thing, the dutiful thing.
We heeded his words, lost as we were for answers.
That day – I grew up. We grew up. We were responsible
for something of consequence, of a precious life,
and no one else could make that decision for us.
You watched as I printed pictures to bury
her with. You dug the hole, shovel in hand, while
the sun reddened your neck. When you thought
we'd said enough, I wanted more – to read an excerpt
from Kipling, from Dickinson, to say a goodbye prayer.

KNIGHT OF CUPS

Lost and alone on Chartres Street
at the witching hour, I happen upon
a mystic who asks to read my tea leaves.
I follow him through red curtains,
down a hallway made of stone
to his tiny room of divination, open
to the living *now* and the living *then*.

My mystic believes in his craft,
sure as bone and blood.
I smell belief on his clothes,
his breath. See it in his glass eye.
He reminds me of Willy Wonka,
both innocent and enterprising.
He's uncommonly benevolent,
prescient to pathways and pinings.

We lean in like old friends.
The space is all shadow,
lit by a candle drowning
in its own wax. I spin the teacup
on the saucer three times,
flip the cup upright.
We peer into the heap of leaves
wet and scattered around the cup's
wide mouth like mazes of mulch,
a garden after a storm: my chaotic
self-portrait only he can discern.

Around us, the French Quarter
hums and swirls with bodies, humidity,
crescendos and accidentals.

This city muddles sin and salvation,
serves the mix blended
with ice in a takeaway chalice.
I never liked the unstirred night,
the darkness. This city answers
my prayer, stays up with me until dawn.

Inside my lonely cup, he interprets
motion, design, hunger, pain.
Very nice, Very nice, he says,
spinning the cup around and around.
His fingers like bulbous seeds
ready for planting, his nail beds
purpling in the season of our session.

Maps papered to my skin. Bodies
of water and land, connected
by long bridges. A journey faraway.
A new face waiting in the distance:
his predictions peel apart my reserves.

He foretells a string of new chapters
beyond the one I'm leaving,
the one I'm already homesick for.
You're gonna be alright girl, he promises
over and over until I almost believe
him, a blend of sass and Southern
on the tongue of this strange, kindred spirit.

Through each curtained door,
I exit the way I came, passing by
the items for sale: tarot cards, rosaries,
incense, clusters of Quartz,
the voodoo dolls: those pained effigies
awaiting their fate in a crowded bowl,
pins piercing all their would-be defenses.

With each step forward, I pull another pin
from my own soft body, dropping each sharp
burden onto the cobblestone below. I remove
the ones I stuck inside, the ones left by others,
watching light fill up every empty wound.

HURRICANE OPHELIA

After the UK storm in 2017

Ophelia in the sky above me,
in the wind that burns my ears.
In this next life, she rises
from the page a tempest, twisting
fearless toward the country
of her creator. No longer
the noble Danish ingénue.
No longer motherless,
fragile, torn between men,
humming words she cannot
speak aloud. Up from the dead,
brought to life in the Sahara sands,
a cyclone savoring the flesh of men.
She grounds planes, knocks the sea
into city walls until the sky goldens.
The crowd on Queen Street stops
to capture scorned Ophelia
with their iPhones. The sun —
red nipple of the forsaken.

EROS THE WINGMAN

Eros is the bro you don't remember friending.
He's just always been around, turning up
to every party late, uninvited, saying he just
dropped by to shoot the shit. Eros is the guy
you've never once asked for advice, yet
he moves the dry red wine over his tongue,
mansplaining to you the proper techniques
for pouring the bottle and tasting the notes
while shamelessly staring at your chest.

Eros introduces himself with twin kisses,
says he's Greek, a primordial god. This usually
garners an uncomfortable laugh, but you're
never quite sure if he's joking or manic.
Eros once told you he loves posters of babies
holding weapons: the good and the bad
of the human world in one image, he says, tearful.
He asks to borrow your phone, and then swipes
right on every guy the app manifests, even
the rugby players who note on their profiles
that they *just can't handle crazy right now.*
You never know, he says, winking at you,
calling out the depths you'd search for love.

As for Eros, he desires cheesepuffs, eats them
by the fistful as he saunters about the flat,
listening in on private conversations.
The cheesepuffs cause the only heartburn
he's ever felt, he jokes. He wipes the orange
crumbs on his tailored three-piece suit
before sneaking to the bathroom to text
a few unprovoked, poorly angled dick pics.

By midnight, he's the life of the party,
reciting the *Kama Sutra* from memory,
using carrot sticks to explain the more complex
configurations. You can't say he isn't
the ultimate wing man, though.
He makes everyone in the room open up, reveal
the desires they bury. With him, they mouth
the word *want* for maybe the first time ever, feel
the electricity of new love pulse around them.

Just before he bids you adieu, Eros catches
your eye, motions to your obnoxious neighbor
who all of a sudden doesn't look so vapid.
Eros winks and takes your hand, spinning your body
like a top toward your next best bad idea.

STARDUST

My gallbladder nearly jumped through the incision
in my skin: troublesome, always cursing the hand that fed it.
It fled inflamed, in a fit of life, was tossed into a surgical waste bin
in Cardiff. Only I ever missed that pouch-like, pear-shaped part of me.
Later, it slipped through an opening in the plastic bag.
Dried up, black, it ended up on the sole of a garbage man's boot.
He thought it aged gum and scraped it off with a razorblade.
I am a student learning to lose myself.

Even before I lost an organ from my singular system,
my wisdom teeth were cut from my jawbone. It was merciless, brutal,
a chop shop my then-husband later recalled. When I awoke, I kept
asking for my teeth, but they hadn't been saved for me.
They had been crooked, growing painfully sideways but they'd been
with me always, relics in my mouth of a life I lived all my own.
If I couldn't wear the four of them about my neck, I wanted
the mere flecks of them from the drill blast, their ruddy trace
on my fingertips. My mouth ached their absence: the empty sockets
hollow and haunted. I was without logic or perspective for weeks.
I only ate mashed potatoes. I left the dust of my teeth
in Louisiana along with so many promises I couldn't keep.

How many selves have I lost? How many selves in those moles
excised from my skin, those precancerous beauty marks
that threatened the number of my days, the one that left
a star-shaped scar on my breast. Or the pink acrylic tips I pulled
one by one from my nail beds on the earliest train from Brighton
to London: tiny plastic petals left where my feet once rested.
I come undone numbering the millions of long blonde strands of hair
I unwittingly let fall behind me. Enough to weave into a scarecrow
who could protect my harvest of cells in today's healthy body.
The eyelashes. The curved, wiry eyebrow threads. I am flanked with grief.

When I walk from room to room, the afternoon light awash through
the windows, my body must look to the microscopic eye
like a shooting star, holy in its naivety, always a ribbon of dead skin,
keratin, atoms, particles shedding from my skin into a streak of life-dust
that fires and trails behind me. I am a student learning to lose myself,
learning to see the elemental, the very physical path my body
has left of me: a path to the past, a path that extends back and back and back:
back to him and through him and through all the mothers who carried me,
back to the burning stars that first envisaged the lovesick idea of me.

THE TRUTH ABOUT LEAVING

So many have asked
when I knew it was over.

They want to know how
to look for it in their own
near-dead relationships.

They want to hear
a foolproof sign
as if I can say:
Look to his skin: look
for the horsehead mole
that sprouts three hairs.

They don't want to hear
that the only revelation
was a dozen tiny pebbles
in our shoes each time
we tried to walk forward.

That we only knew
we couldn't continue.

They don't want to hear
that certainty never came.
That sufficient closure
might be a myth.

That I still look for
posthumous signs.

That I still wonder
if we did our best.

ACRYLIC DREAM

I don't blame you for leaving
me in the past, but the absence
of your voice makes the dreams
of you frequent, stranger.
Last night, your mother made
a nursery for us, wallpapered
the lonely room a color I didn't
have a name for. Hung gold
mirrors from ceiling to floor.
We lived in the woods by a dam.
The trees were made of acrylic
paint, didn't grow or dry.
In our old kayaks, we paddled
foolishly to the edge
of the dam's open mouth.
We knew we were done for.
Just before we went over
the falls, you took my hand,
assured me I was only dreaming.
Your confidence soothing my
fear even now, even in my sleep.
Later, we pulled ourselves ashore,
walked home with broken feet.
All the while, the child we wanted
someday, that we named Hadley
or Elias, cried for us in the trees.

MERMAIDS

What do we forget when we tell
ourselves that mermaids
are mere folklore, explained away
as manatees or dugongs, species
in the order of Sirenia?

We forget the condition
called syndactyly. The webbing
of human flesh, hiding under
gloves, closed-toe shoes.

We forget sirenomelia –
known as mermaid syndrome –
that legs can fuse together
in utero, longing for the sea.

We forget ourselves. We forget
that all daughters are mermaids,
that all sons are mermen,
having once been sealed
three quarters of a year
in the ocean of our mothers.

THE FAMILIAR

My cat arranged the tiny victim of her kill
onto my bedroom floor – an offering gladly divided
into head, torso, wing – before curling onto the backs
of my legs to sleep once more.

Years ago, she came to me. A calico, tabby mix. A stray.
I've heard it said that cats choose their owners.
She'd manifested in our apartment courtyard.
Followed me on walks. Sat at our door in submission
while I fumbled with my keys, asking to be mine.

On our patio that autumn, she birthed a litter of four kittens
that she and I cared for together, she a near-kitten herself.
Then came an infection from a botfly that nearly killed her.
The vet had to gut her throat. *She's a stray*, I'd said.
I'm not so sure she is anymore, the vet replied.

But even when she'd been accepted as ours, domesticity
never quite suited. Indoor life wore heavy on her,
like a coat with rocks sown into the seams.
She'd leave for days and return dazed, a redness
clouding her green eyes. She'd known the wild once more.

You're her pack leader, he said. *She stopped coming home
after you left.* By then, we'd also faced the Great Flood
of Baton Rouge, a divorce. I was back to claim her,
and she came running home when I called her name,
rode on my lap the whole drive out of Louisiana.

Just last night I stroked her head and confided in her
that I didn't think I had another poem in me,
that all those hurts, the doubts had taken from me
a fundamental calling. She yawned, twitched her ears.

I found a latex glove and a Wal-Mart bag with which
to rid my bedroom of the dead bird. But when I returned,
my cat was wide awake, chewing at the side of its torso,
a dark feather hanging from her mouth. I stood horrified
but couldn't look away. How she accepted her own true nature.
How she protected it, savored it. How she made no apologies.

Night has fallen on us again. Head, torso, wing. I can't
get the image out of my mind, how she had the parts
of the bird already broken into pieces, placed into a strange
triangle, awaiting my waking, my horror, my intrigue.

Head, torso, wing. I think now she must have known
I couldn't not write about it. This dark offering of hers.

THE ART OF LETTING GO

Nothing is truly lost.
I see that now.
All those times we talked
about the first law of
thermodynamics you studied
in your engineering classes –
that *energy cannot be created
or destroyed* – what if we had
made the connection sooner?
Seen ourselves as part
of that same energy?
Then, we would have known
that we never truly began,
never ended. That our story
lives on as it always has.

MOONSTRUCK

My new lover wants me to watch as he peels
from his eyelids the strips of his dark lashes.
I find them later on his bedside table, blinking
one atop the other, bristles sharp as caterpillars.

Outside the window, the world continues to dim.
For years, a new moon hovered in the sky, obscuring
the faces, the once familiar valleys and vistas.

The next night my new lover removes his teeth.
One by one from his jaw, he twists each tooth
from its vine like a ripe grape, lets each drop
into the tiny porcelain dish on his boudoir.
His voice changes after but it does not age him.

I go to his window again and find what looks
like hope: a tender sliver of light in the sky, curved –
the makings of a crescent moon.

On the third night we make love. After, he perfects
the art of coming undone, hanging his curly mop
of hair from the banister. He appears taller
without hair and truer. The indents, grooves of his
skull revealing his tough, his fragile humanity.

Outside, the night has brightened: a first quarter
half-moon. The sky studded with tinfoil stars.
I rest my cheek on his soft shoulder
as we look out onto our moonlit metropolis.

The more I come to know him, the more he reveals
to me his secret celestial cycle. By the time

he asks for my help lifting off his skin, I reach
my hands to him instinctively. I ask no questions.
We hang his skin in the closet around a hanger
like a garment bag. I behold his new form,
knowing then the raw bone and blood of him.

Nothing seems impossible anymore,
not on the night he asks for my help unclipping
his tongue and then dislodging his kind eyes.
Without his tongue, his spoken words become
guttural but glad. His eyes now free to roll
about our realm, see in full panoramic rotation.

In his own time and with my help, my new lover
and I deconstruct every part of him, each piece
of his puzzle put away in its own drawer, box,
jar, dish. His memories organized in file folders.
We rest together in the bed we now share, his
remaining form a mere kernel of light in my arms
under the brightest harvest moon the world's ever
witnessed. Too bright to look backwards or to grieve.

ST. FAGAN'S MUSEUM OF WELSH LIFE

For Martyn

At the St. Fagan's Museum of Welsh Life,
we study each other as much as the exhibits.
We sip cool white wine from a Swell bottle,
ask each other daring questions, allow our
shoulders to graze one another's. We grin.
He teaches me the Welsh word *cwtch*,
for the kind of hug that feels like home.
I ponder at his Welsh prepositions: *by there*,
he says pointing to another path in the distance.
We wander from dwelling to dwelling, each
from a different Welsh town, time period.
He thinks of the word *hiraeth*, says it's
a Welsh concept of homesickness, a longing
for a place to which one cannot return.
Just then, I feel the page turn to a new chapter.
It's only our third date, but he makes me want
to pick flowers again to dry and to keep.
He makes me want to pack a blanket, savor
the new daffodils yielding to the spring wind.
With him, I feel the sun even in my pulse,
warming my wintered skin. With him,
anywhere and everywhere could be home.

ACKNOWLEDGEMENTS

Whenever a project comes to a close, I am always so grateful to the people who helped make the work possible. No one accomplishes anything alone; there is always a network of people involved in the creation of anything worthwhile.

Firstly, I am so thankful to Erna Kuik for agreeing to collaborate with me and allowing the use of her images in this book and on the cover. The genesis of the collaboration between Erna's artwork and my poems began as most good things do: with a chance meeting. I didn't plan on being at the Art Amsterdam Spui on a cold December afternoon in Amsterdam. But, when I turned the corner and saw Erna's artwork at her market booth, I was stunned. I felt as though I was looking at the visual counterparts to my poems, even though Erna and I had never met. I believe Erna and I are kindred spirits, both forever wrestling connections of the past, the what ifs, and yet both so committed to female autonomy, personal growth, magic, art, words, and creative living. In total, the collaboration comprises the 11 poem/image pairings found in this book. It has been an honor to work with you, Erna. *Heel erg bedankt!*

I am grateful to the editors at the following publications, where many of the poems in this manuscript first appeared:

Canyon Voice: 'Girl Talk' and 'Dear Reader, Love Poet'.
Les Femmes Folles: 'How to Build a Dock' with image by Erna Kuik and a reprint of 'Dear Reader, Love Poet' with image by Erna Kuik.
Phantom Drift: 'Another Night on Bourbon Street'.
Poetica Review: 'Kintsugi' and 'The Truth About Leaving'.
Poetry South: 'Honeybees'.

So to Speak: 'Whole Nine Yards'.

Stirring: 'Moonstruck'.

Sylvia Magazine: 'Summer Blues'.

The Cardiff Review: 'Dear Blue Pill' with image by Erna Kuik and 'Dear Depression' with image by Erna Kuik.

The Ekphrastic Review: 'Nesting' with image by Erna Kuik and a reprint of 'Girl Talk' with image by Erna Kuik.

Wicked Alice: 'Ovarian Teratoma' and 'Glory'.

Thanks to Kristy Bowen and Dancing Girl Press for publishing my chapbook titled *Along the Diminishing Stretch of Memory* in 2014. A few of the poems in this collection appeared in this chapbook.

Thanks to the editorial team at Eyewear/Black Spring Press Group for editing and publishing this collection. A special thanks to Todd Swift, Cate Myddleton-Evans, Amira Ghanim, and Edwin Smet.

Thanks to Catherine Pierce, Kathy Fagan, and Claire Williamson for their generous endorsements of this book.

Thanks to the faculty and my peers at Mississippi State University, The University of Louisiana at Lafayette, and Cardiff University, especially Catherine Pierce, Richard Lyons, and Richard Gwyn.

Thanks to dear friends who helped me make the biggest transition of my life. I literally couldn't have done it without you: Lauren Dodd, Kevin Armstrong, Wade Spurlock, Christina Thatcher, Rich Daly, Julie Primon Axtell, Richard Axtell, Anna Marie Young, Julia Rose Lewis, and Kedar Naik.

Thanks to Matt Christian. Though our journeys took us in separate directions, I wouldn't be who I am without the years we spent together.

Thank to my parents, Charles and Kathy Collins, for supporting me my entire life, for their love, and for their never-ending interest in my writing.

And finally, thanks to Martyn White – My light. My peace. My home.

ARTIST'S STATEMENT BY ERNA KUIK

While you are reading this, I am probably cutting and inking my linocuts and turning the wheel of my press. Her name is Rolls by the way. I fill each work with good intentions, vibrant colours and forms, to let it sparkle.

I think you recognise the feeling you had when you were a child, gazing at clouds, stars or simply the ceiling of your room. Thinking about 'everything.' This enchantment is exactly why I make art. Phenomena and feelings that cannot be explained in rational terms, can move and touch us deeply. Imagination helps me to find forms to express my impressions. And words too – they are worlds in themselves. The powerful combination of text and images connects me with the wonder of our existence.

We are standing on the shoulders of our ancestors; ideas and thoughts are passed on again and again, and they gradually change form. To me, art is a kind of relay race or a parallel universe in which universal wisdom is shared. When I remember my dreams while working, I know that I am on the right track.

At the Artez Art Academy, I learned a lot about observing. I chose the Free Graphics course and learned a true craft: printing. A line becomes more interesting when converted into a linocut or woodcut. It gains power and expression; the gouge makes a line whimsical.

I like portraying people as thinkers and dreamers. In one of my works featured in this collection, a young woman sits at a table. A cup has fallen over the table; the water flows out. The young woman stares either at a kind of empty space, to the observer, or to her inner world. The water becomes a metaphor for the flow of information that we have to process. It has become increasingly clear to me that 'doing nothing' is also doing a lot. We could take the time to look at the void, so we make room for the thoughts within ourselves. Time passes by slower, and our observation deepens. The impressions we collect are *une mer à boire,* a sea to drink.

In my work, I aim to give voice to everyday moments.

I partly make my own paper out of old magazines. In fact, many of the images in this collaboration were created using this handmade paper. Nothing can beat this gorgeous paper, with its pretty jagged edges and added collages. It is very satisfying to make something so beautiful out of waste material. I have my own paper recycling factory and especially during summer with warm weather, papermaking is very refreshing. 'Worthless' material is the most honorable material. The combination of linoprint on collaged hand-made paper makes every print an exclusive one.

'For I am part of nature' is my key theme at the moment. Caring for nature is also caring for yourself. Plants, animals and humans; it's the real 'us'. Let's think inclusive all together.

Erna Kuik in her studio in The Netherlands, 2021. Photo by Corrie Kuik-Buizer.

CHRISTIE COLLINS was born and raised in the American South, and she has recently moved back to Mississippi after a decade away. She currently teaches courses in writing and literature at Mississippi State University in Starkville, Mississippi. Prior to her return home, she lived in Cardiff, Wales, where she completed a Ph.D. in Critical and Creative Writing at Cardiff University. She has also taught at Louisiana State University and Cardiff University. Her critical and creative work has been published in *Stirring, Phantom Drift, Kenyon Review Online, North Carolina Literary Review, Entropy, Cold Mountain Review, Appalachian Heritage, Poetry South, Poetry Wales, Still: The Journal, So to Speak* among others. Her chapbook titled *Along the Diminishing Stretch of Memory* was published in 2014 by Dancing Girl Press. Christie's creative work often focuses on questions of place, belonging, and connection, on visual art and a predilection for ekphrastic projects, and on finding a magic, otherworldly spark in the seemingly unremarkable.

ERNA KUIK is a photographer, visual artist, and writer from the Netherlands. After graduating from the Artez Academy in 1992, her artwork was awarded the Gretha and Adri Pieck Prize, an award to encourage young, promising artists. Her work tends to an expressionistic style, known for its strong lines in linocuts and its poetic content. She wrote and illustrated children's books about very creative hares published by Atlantie Verlag Switzerland and has published other work that features her photography and illustrations. Her art can be found in many private collections worldwide and is exhibited in museums like the Kunstmuseum in The Hague, Museum De Fundatie in Zwolle and in several galleries. She loves to be in her studio; the spirit of making fluid thoughts into sparkling crystals on paper keeps her going.